SPACE!

URANUS

JOSEPHA SHERMAN

Marshall Cavendish
Benchmark
New York

Marshall Cavendish Benchmark
99 White Plains Road
Tarrytown, New York 10591
www.marshallcavendish.us

Library of Congress Cataloging-in-Publication Data
Sherman, Josepha.
  Uranus / by Josepha Sherman.
     p. cm. -- (Space!)
  Summary: "Describes Uranus, including its history, its composition, and its role in the
solar system"--Provided by publisher.
  Includes bibliographical references and index.
  ISBN 978-0-7614-4248-6
  1. Uranus (Planet)--Juvenile literature. 2. Herschel, William, Sir, 1738-1822--Juvenile
literature. I. Title.
  QB681.S54 2010
  523.47--dc22
  2008037274

Editor: Karen Ang
Publisher: Michelle Bisson
Art Director: Anahid Hamparian
Series Design by Daniel Roode
Production by nSight, Inc.

Front cover: A computer illustration of Uranus
Title page: A spacecraft does a flyby past Uranus.
Photo research by Candlepants, Inc.
Front cover: Chris Bjornberg / Photo Researchers Inc.
The photographs in this book are used by permission and through the courtesy of:
Corbis: 1; Bettmann, 30. Super Stock: Digital Vision Ltd., 4, 5. The Image Works: SSPL, 7,
11; Mary Evans Picture Library, 13(right). Getty Images: Time & Life Pictures, 8, 32; Kauko
Helavuo, 16; AFP, 22; National Geographic, 29(lower), 41; 23, 35, 38, 49; Joe McNally, 52.
NASA: A. Zezas and J. Huchra (Harvard-Smithsonian Center for Astrophysics), 13(left);
JPL, 20, 28-29, 31, 34, 37, 40; JPL/STScI,50, 58. New York Public Library: Picture Collection,
Astor, Lenox and Tilden Foundations, 14. Photo Researchers Inc.: Roger Harris, 18, 19;
Mark Garlick, 25, 36, 42, 43, 46; California Association for Research in Astronomy, 57.
Calvin J. Hamilton: 26, 27. AP Images: NASA, 53. European Space Agency: 55. Illustration
on page 45 by Mapping Specialists © Marshall Cavendish.
Printed in Malaysia
123456

CONTENTS

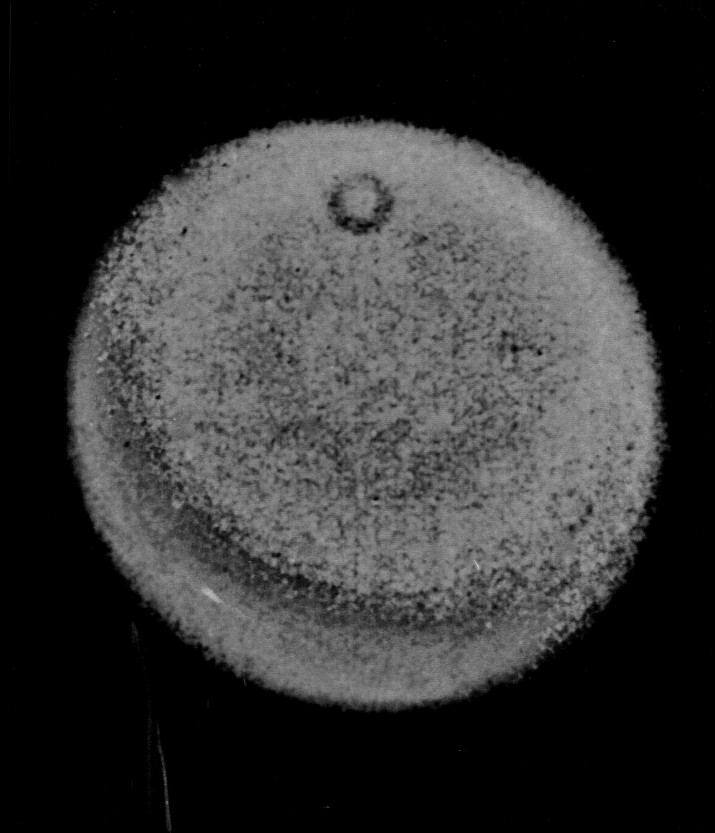

1

AN UNEXPECTED DISCOVERY

In the eighteenth century, people believed that there were only six planets in our Solar System. These planets were Mercury, Venus, Earth, Mars, Jupiter, and Saturn. No new planets had been discovered for nearly two thousand years because the technology was not good enough.

With the observation equipment available at that time, no one could search deeply into space. People had long been interested in objects in space, but **astronomy** was still a new science in the eighteenth century. There were no such things as ready-made telescopes available in markets. Scientists had to make their own. Anyone wanting to see the stars through a telescope had to either be very good at making things, such as grinding glass lenses, or rich enough to get someone to make a telescope for him or her.

Scientists did not know about Uranus's many features until the creation of powerful telescopes and spacecraft that could travel near the planet. This image of Uranus was taken by the *Voyager 2* spacecraft in 1986.

THE MUSICAL ASTRONOMER

William Herschel had never really expected to be an **astronomer**. Born on November 15, 1738, as Friedrich Wilhelm Herschel, he was part of a musical family in Germany. At first, he fully intended to follow in the family tradition. He became a fine singer, and his sister Caroline often joined him in duets. Then Herschel's life changed dramatically. He tried military life as a teenager, but realized that he did not want to stay in the military. In 1757, at the age of nineteen, Herschel left Germany forever. He had visited England once and liked it, and he could already speak English, so he headed there.

Herschel became a British citizen and changed his name from Friedrich Wilhelm Herschel to the more English-sounding Frederick William Herschel. He took a job as a music teacher to make a living, performing the violin, the oboe, and the organ. The busy Herschel also composed music. In 1772, he persuaded his sister, Caroline, also interested in music, to join him in England.

Music is made up of specific beats and notes, and Herschel and his sister began to study mathematics to help him with his compositions. Through mathematics they became fascinated with the relatively new science of astronomy. Among the books that they owned were Robert Smith's 1738 book, *The Compleat System of Optiks*—the branch of science that deals with the properties of light—and James Ferguson's 1756 book, *Astronomy*.

THE TELESCOPES OF HERSCHEL'S TIME

The first reflecting telescope was designed by the Scottish scientist James Gregory, who lived in the 1600s. But it was not a perfectly working device. The next effective telescope inventors were two English scientists from the seventeenth century. Robert Hooke was noted for both his telescopes and microscopes, and Sir Isaac Newton was an astronomer, mathematician, and physicist. Then, in the 1720s, Englishman John Hadley, with the help of his brothers George and Henry, built the first useful reflecting telescopes. Since he made a thorough study of the science of optics and telescopes, Herschel would have known about all of these and used that knowledge when building his own telescopes.

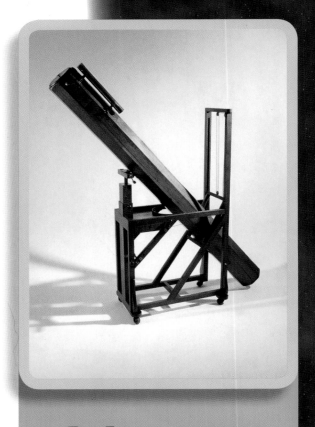

This 7-foot-long telescope was made in 1783 by William Herschel.

Herschel and his sister Caroline used telescopes to chart the features and movement of different celestial bodies.

Herschel was quoted as saying, "Among other mathematical subjects astronomy came in turn . . . I was so delighted with the subject that I wished to see the heavens and planets with my own eyes thro' [a telescope]." This meant that, like all the other astronomers of his time, Herschel had to build his own telescope. He read Smith's book from cover to cover and studied all he could learn about optics and the making of telescope lenses, and then he put together several test telescopes. Herschel finally built such a good telescope that even the professional astronomers at London's Royal Observatory announced that they could not make a better one. Herschel's telescope is a reflecting telescope, which magnifies far-off objects using mirrors rather than glass lenses. Light enters the telescope and is reflected twice before it enters the eyepiece.

Music—and getting paid for his music—was still Herschel's way of making a living. However, his spare time was now completely filled with his astronomical observations. Herschel had quickly realized that no one had made a comprehensive celestial atlas—an atlas of all the objects in space. Herschel's goal was to make one. He was particularly interested in making a catalog of double stars, which are two stars that seem to be almost in line. Herschel was planning to use the data he was collecting to calculate the distance from Earth to a star, something no one had ever been able to do.

In 1781, Herschel began spending each night making a careful, measured study of a different part of the sky, marking down everything he saw in each section. He saw single and double stars, comets, and five of the six known planets—Mercury, Venus, Mars, Jupiter, and Saturn. Everything seemed in order.

A SURPRISE DISCOVERY

Then on March 13, 1781, Herschel found a strange object in the night sky that did not seem to fit the regular pattern. It did not move or act like a star. At first, he thought that what he was seeing had to be either a comet or a nebulous star, which is a star that is seen through a **nebula**, or a dust cloud in space. It did not occur to Herschel that he had found a new planet. He told other astronomers about what he had found, and they, too, thought it surely was only a comet.

By the summer of 1781, more detailed observations were made by another astronomer, Anders Johann Lexell. Other astronomers made their calculations as well. It was proven that this strange object **orbited** around the Sun, just like other planets. Herschel had indeed discovered that there was a seventh planet in the Solar System.

The news was truly amazing. It was in all the newspapers and in everyone's conversations. The size of our Solar System had suddenly doubled, and it now seemed almost unbelievably

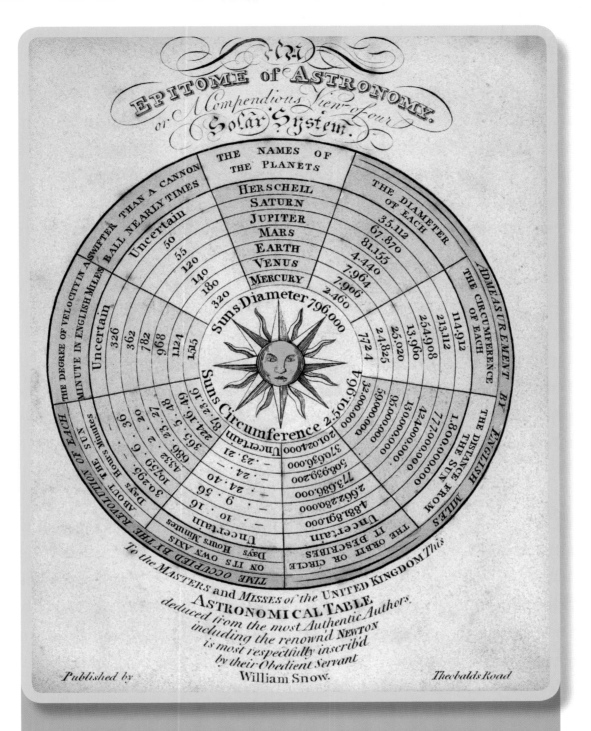

An eighteenth-century planetary chart shows the recorded features and characteristics of the seven known planets. Here, Uranus is called "Herschel."

big. Uranus was as far from the sixth planet, Saturn, as Saturn was from Earth. All the information about our Solar System now had to be updated. As further studies of Uranus were made, astronomers realized that previous scholars had noticed it as far back as 1690. But those earlier astronomers were using weaker telescopes, and they all thought that what they saw was just another star.

Scientists around the world praised Herschel for his discovery. King George III knighted Herschel and gave him and Caroline the titles of "The King's Astronomer" and "Assistant to the King's Astronomer," an honor which came with a lifetime salary for them both. He also gave them their own private observatory. Now Herschel and his sister were free to become full-time astronomers. Herschel also became a telescope maker.

Naming the Planet

At first, no one knew what to name this new planet. Herschel wanted to name it *Georgium Sidus*, or George's Star, after King George III of England, who was giving Herschel money for his studies of astronomy. None of the other astronomers really liked that name, particularly since what had been found was a planet, not a star. Some astronomers wanted to call it Herschel after its discoverer, but that did not catch on.

JOHANN BODE

German astronomer Johann Elert Bode also became interested in astronomy through mathematics. In late 1774, Bode began looking for star clusters in the sky, and observed twenty of them. Among his finds are three original discoveries: M81 (also known as Bode's Galaxy) and M82, both of which he discovered on December 31, 1774; and M53, which he discovered on February 3, 1775. He discovered numerous other star clusters and helped to calculate the orbit of Uranus.

Johann Bode

M81, or Bode's Galaxy, viewed from the Hubble Space Telescope.

An artist's depiction of Uranus, from whom all other gods and goddesses descended.

Finally, Johann Bode pointed out that the other planets had mythological names, such as Saturn and Jupiter. Bode thought that the new planet should be named Uranus. In Greek and Roman mythology, Uranus was known as the god of the sky. Most of the other Greek and Roman gods and goddesses descended from Uranus.

Some of the other astronomers agreed with the suggested name, while others did not. Some astronomers called it "the

Georgian planet," and still others called it "Herschel." It took a full sixty years of arguing over the name before astronomers agreed to call the seventh planet Uranus.

ANOTHER SURPRISE DISCOVERY

In 1787, Herschel made another discovery about Uranus. He found two moons orbiting it. By that time, not all celestial bodies were being named after Roman mythology. As a result, Herschel's two moons were named Titania and Oberon. Those were the names of the queen and king of fairies in William Shakespeare's play *A Midsummer Night's Dream*.

Herschel thought that there might be four other moons orbiting Uranus, but he could not find any way to prove it. The trouble was that even though Herschel was building some of the finest and largest telescopes in the world, there was still a great deal that he simply could not see. The distances were too great and even the best telescopes of the time were not very strong. The images were just too faint for him to make accurate calculations. Herschel also thought that he had glimpsed rings around the planet, like the rings of Saturn. However, since the image he saw was so blurry, he suspected that the "rings" were just a trick of the light.

An artist's illustration shows how the young planet Uranus might have been struck by a large object, like an asteroid, causing the planet to tilt.

There was one more surprise for William Herschel and his fellow eighteenth-century astronomers. When they studied the orbits of Oberon and Titania they expected to find that the two moons orbited around Uranus's equator. (That is where our Moon and the other planets' moons orbit.) But that did not work out for Oberon and Titania because Uranus's equator appeared to be different from equators of other planets. This meant that Uranus was tilted onto its side, with its North Pole on one end and the South Pole at the other. None of the other planets the astronomers had studied had more than a small tilt. What could have happened to Uranus? They could only guess that a large body, maybe a huge **asteroid**, had slammed into the planet and tilted it. That theory never has been proved or disproved.

2

THE MYSTERY PLANET

Uranus remained a mystery planet for more than a century after it was discovered. The biggest problem—even though telescopes were slowly improving—was the great distance between Earth and Uranus. Even when it is as close to Earth as its orbit allows and viewed through a good telescope, Uranus seems to be a disk with a diameter of only about 4 inches (10 centimeters.) There is a good reason for this. Uranus is about 1.69 billion miles (2.72 billion kilometers) from Earth. This is more than eighteen times as far as the distance between Earth and the Sun.

More Uranus discoveries were made in the nineteenth century. British astronomer William Lassell found two more of Uranus's moons in 1851. He named them Ariel and Umbriel. The

As the seventh planet from the Sun, it is not surprising that Uranus can be difficult to see from Earth, which is only the third planet from the Sun.

19

Miranda was first noticed in 1948, but obtaining detailed images of the moon's surface only became possible when the spacecraft *Voyager 2* flew by Uranus in the 1980s.

name Ariel is from Shakespeare's works, and follows the theme used in naming Titania and Oberon. However, Umbriel is a character in a poem by English poet Alexander Pope.

After Lassell's discovery, there came another long stretch of time where nothing new was learned about Uranus. In 1948, American astronomer Gerard Peter Kuiper discovered another moon orbiting Uranus. He named it Miranda, which is another name taken from Shakespeare. It was thought at the time of discovery—since no one could prove otherwise—that Miranda was the moon closest to Uranus. It would be years before more information was discovered.

THE SPACE RACE

A combination of scientific curiosity and international problems brought about a new space organization for the United States, and a new chance for astronomers to make discoveries. The United States had been thinking about going into space and exploring it for years. One of the main reasons was curiosity, but the other reason was the Cold War. That was a war without fighting between the United States and what was then the Soviet Union, made up of Russia and its conquered countries. As part of the Cold War, the United States and the Soviet Union became involved in a "space race," mostly to see who would be the first to land a man on the Moon.

In 1957, the Soviet Union launched *Sputnik 1,* the first artificial **satellite**. That spurred the United States to action. In 1958, NASA, the National Aeronautics and Space Administration, was formed. Its mission was to achieve great scientific and technical goals in the air and in space. Among those goals were manned space flight, and the landing of men on the Moon. Thanks to NASA, men did land on the Moon several times, from 1969 to 1972.

There were many other missions that the scientists at NASA wanted to accomplish. Scientists at the agency wanted to know more about the Solar System. Unfortunately, most of the planets were just too far away for manned missions. A person would die of old age long before he or she ever reached the outer planets in a spacecraft. Scientists had to mostly rely on satellites and other Earth- or space-based telescopes for information about and images from outer space.

THE COLD WAR

This is the name for the era of competition and tension between the United States and the Soviet Union, and both sides' allies. It lasted from about 1945 until the early 1990s. The United States and the Soviet Union "fought" the cold war in many ways, including spying, military buildups, a dangerous nuclear weapons race, and the space race. Today, the United States and Russia are allies in the space program, and are both involved in the construction of the International Space Station.

In addition to launching the first artificial satellite, the Soviet Union was also the first to send a living creature into space. The dog named Laika was sent into space in 1957.

VOYAGER 1 AND VOYAGER 2

Planets like Uranus were too far away for any manned missions, but NASA began planning for two related unmanned missions to visit far-off planets. They began work on the design of twin spacecraft, named *Voyager 1* and *Voyager 2*.

At the time, the two spacecraft, identical in every aspect, were two of the most sophisticated robot crafts ever built. Each carried its own power and propulsion, as well as scientific instruments and communications systems that would keep them

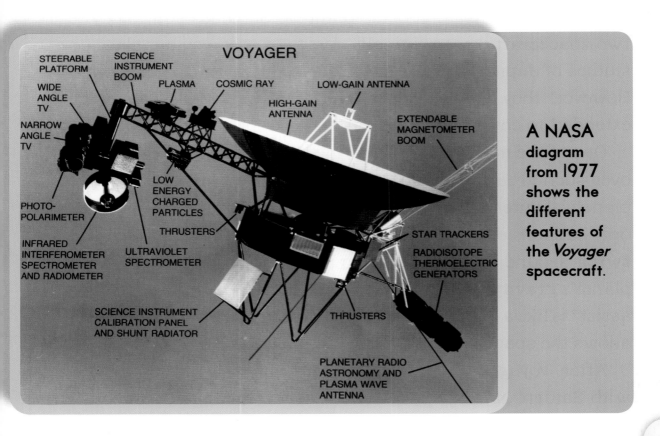

VOYAGER

STEERABLE PLATFORM
SCIENCE INSTRUMENT BOOM
PLASMA
COSMIC RAY
LOW-GAIN ANTENNA
WIDE ANGLE TV
HIGH-GAIN ANTENNA
NARROW ANGLE TV
EXTENDABLE MAGNETOMETER BOOM
LOW ENERGY CHARGED PARTICLES
PHOTO-POLARIMETER
THRUSTERS
STAR TRACKERS
INFRARED INTERFEROMETER SPECTROMETER AND RADIOMETER
ULTRAVIOLET SPECTROMETER
RADIOISOTOPE THERMOELECTRIC GENERATORS
SCIENCE INSTRUMENT CALIBRATION PANEL AND SHUNT RADIATOR
THRUSTERS
PLANETARY RADIO ASTRONOMY AND PLASMA WAVE ANTENNA

A NASA diagram from 1977 shows the different features of the *Voyager* spacecraft.

in touch with the NASA scientists on Earth. Each *Voyager* had a series of connected computer "brains" that allowed the craft to operate on its own for weeks. The "brains" even included the ability to find and correct errors before the NASA scientists were aware of them. Everyone hoped that the two spacecraft would finally answer some questions about the more distant planets in our Solar System, including Uranus.

The twin *Voyagers* were launched in summer of 1977 from the NASA Kennedy Space Center at Cape Canaveral, Florida. *Voyager 2* was launched first, on August 20, 1977. *Voyager 1* was launched on a faster, shorter flight on September 5, 1977. The two spacecraft were originally designed to carry out close-up studies of Jupiter and Saturn and those planets' larger moons. However, they performed so well that their missions were extended to cover visits to Uranus and Neptune as well.

One of the main reasons that the missions could be extended over such great distances was a rare arrangement of the four planets, Jupiter, Saturn, Uranus, and Neptune. This arrangement only happens every 175 years. It meant that a spacecraft could swing around one planet to the next, taking advantage of one planet's **gravity** to move it to the next planet. This "gravitational assist" is like a slingshot adding extra speed to a spacecraft. This allows the spacecraft to travel without too much extra fuel.

After *Voyager 2* had carried out its successful encounter with Saturn, NASA scientists were certain that the spacecraft

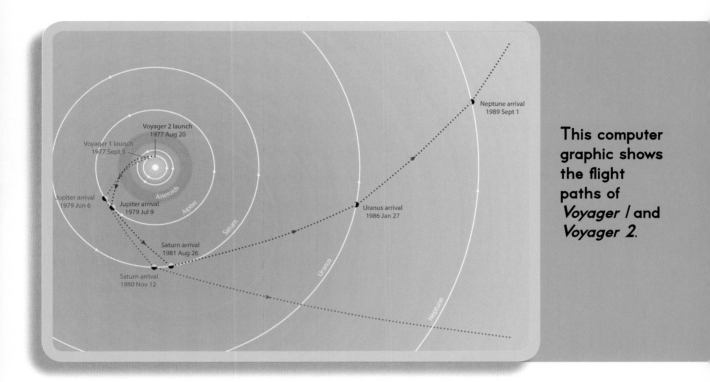

Voyager 2 launch
1977 Aug 20

Voyager 1 launch
1977 Sept 5

Jupiter arrival
1979 Jun 6

Jupiter arrival
1979 Jul 9

Asteroids

Jupiter

Saturn

Saturn arrival
1981 Aug 26

Saturn arrival
1980 Nov 12

Uranus arrival
1986 Jan 27

Uranus

Neptune arrival
1989 Sept 1

Neptune

This computer graphic shows the flight paths of *Voyager 1* and *Voyager 2*.

would be able to fly on to Uranus with all its systems functioning. While *Voyager 1* set out to conduct studies of outer space, and will eventually leave our star system completely, *Voyager 2*'s meeting with Uranus began in the 1980s.

To prepare for the flyby of Uranus, NASA engineers on Earth did some major reprogramming of the spacecraft's onboard computers. These changes would let *Voyager 2* take and send clear photographs even though the great distance from the Sun meant that there was little light. In addition, giant antenna receiving stations on Earth were linked electronically to be sure they could catch *Voyager 2*'s faint radio signal.

3
NEW DISCOVERIES

URANUS'S MOONS

To scientists' delight and relief, *Voyager 2* took clear, sharp pictures of the five large moons of Uranus. These were Miranda, Ariel, Umbriel, Titania, and Oberon. The two largest, Titania and Oberon, are about 1,000 miles (1,600 km) in diameter. This means that they are about half the size of Earth's Moon. The smallest of the five, Miranda, is only 300 miles (500 km) in diameter. These five moons, judging from the information that *Voyager 2* sent back, are made of a mix of ice and rock. Titania and Oberon may be as much as 50 percent ice, 20 percent frozen chemicals and minerals, and 30 percent rock. *Voyager 2* also discovered ten new moons, including one that scientists named Puck. Puck is only about 90 miles (150 km) in diameter, but that makes it larger than many asteroids.

This image of Uranus was taken by *Voyager 2*.

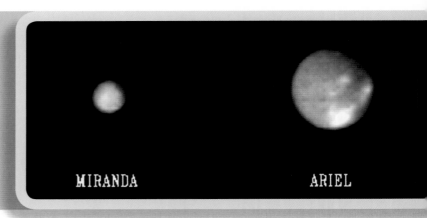

This "family portrait" of some of Uranus's moons is made up of different images that *Voyager 2* took in 1986.

MIRANDA   ARIEL

Finding any of Uranus's moons is difficult. Many of them are tiny, some with diameters less than 10 miles (16 km) and nearly black in color. While *Voyager 2* sent back information about the inner moons and their composition, even now no one knows very much about the outer moons. Scientists think that these outer moons may actually be asteroids. These large rocks might have been caught by Uranus's gravity and ended up in permanent orbit around the planet.

Miranda

Miranda, named for a character in Shakespeare's play, *The Tempest,* is the innermost and smallest of the five major moons. It is also one of the strangest of Uranus's moons. In fact, its surface is not like anything else found in the Solar System so far. The moon looks as though it had been jumbled together. Miranda has giant fault canyons deeper than the Grand Canyon, many terrace-like

UMBRIEL   TITANIA   OBERON

layers, surfaces that appear very old, and other surfaces that look much younger. Scientists are not sure what happened to Miranda to make it like this. It might have been turned almost

inside out by the strong forces of gravity from Uranus and the other moons. Another theory is that Miranda might have been shattered in a collision with another moon or an asteroid and then reassembled by Uranus's gravity. Because it is a fairly small moon, all that activity still has scientists puzzled.

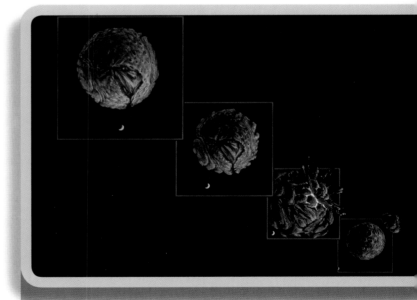

An asteroid or some form of space debris might have come near Miranda and struck it (bottom right), causing the moon's uneven surface and shape (upper left).

Gerard Kuiper was a Dutch-American astronomer who is responsible for many important space discoveries. He was the first to discover Miranda. Kuiper also discovered Nereid, a moon of the planet Neptune. His research on planetary atmospheres discovered that carbon dioxide was in the atmosphere of Mars and a methane-rich atmosphere was above Saturn's moon Titan. Kuiper also participated in the NASA program to land humans on the Moon. He believed that there was a stretch of outer space beyond our Solar System that contained small planets, space debris, and the beginnings of comets. Today, most scientists call this area the Kuiper Belt. These are just some of Kuiper's many important astronomical discoveries. Because he was so respected in his field, NASA's KAO (Kuiper Airborne Observatory) was named for him, and the Kuiper Prize is a very important astronomy award that is given to scientists who contribute to our knowledge of space.

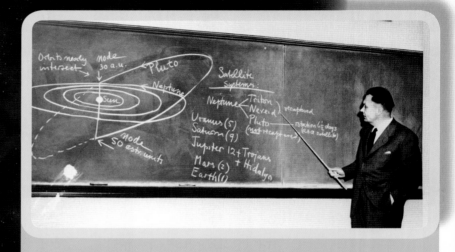

Gerard Kuiper also believed that Pluto was a satellite of Neptune, and not a full-sized planet. Today, Pluto is considered a dwarf planet, different from the other planets in our Solar System.

Ariel and Umbriel

Ariel is also named after a character in *The Tempest*. This moon may have the youngest and brightest surface of Uranus's moons. While it has many small craters, it has only a few large ones. This may mean that many low-impact collisions gradually destroyed any larger craters. The only other scars on Ariel's surface are long valleys. Scientists think that there may be some signs of early ice or, possibly, lava flows in those valleys.

Named for a character in an Alexander Pope poem, Umbriel is the darkest of the moons. The darkness of its surface is probably a result of many major impacts. Umbriel is covered with large old craters—but it also has a mysterious bright ring on one side that scientists cannot explain.

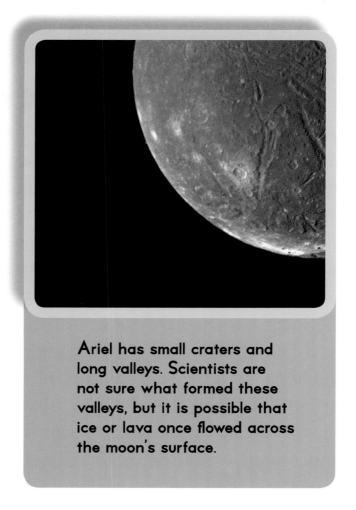

Ariel has small craters and long valleys. Scientists are not sure what formed these valleys, but it is possible that ice or lava once flowed across the moon's surface.

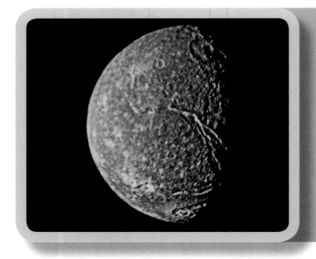

Voyager 2 was able to show scientists the surface of Titania, which has many canyons and fault lines.

Titania and Oberon

Titania is the largest of Uranus's moons, with a diameter of 998 miles (1,500 km). It has long canyons and **fault lines** that might mean that some violent movement took place in its **crust** sometime in its past. These canyons and lines might have been caused by ice forcing apart the surface long ago, or by erosion, which is the wearing away of the surface over time by natural forces.

Oberon is the furthest out of the five major moons. It is old and heavily cratered. There does not seem to be any internal **geologic** activity, such as violent movements or shifts in the crust and inner layers. There is some unknown dark material on the floors of many of Oberon's craters. That may be some inner matter that came to the surface in the past, when the moon still did have any geologic activity.

Cordelia and Ophelia

These small moons are also both named for characters in Shakespeare's plays. Not much is known about their appearance because they are so small. They are known as "shepherd moons." These are moons that sort of anchor Uranus's outermost ring with their gravity and keep it from falling apart.

The Eight Small Moons

Between Miranda and the two shepherd moons lies a crowded tangle of eight small satellites that are completely different from any other system of planetary moons. In fact, they are so crowded that astronomers do not know how the moons manage to keep from crashing into each other. They may be shepherds for the planet's ten narrow rings. Scientists think that there may be more tiny moons helping to hold together the edges of the inner rings. So far, though, no more of them have been found.

A RINGED PLANET

On March 11, 1977—before *Voyager 2* was launched—scientists noticed objects around Uranus that resembled Saturn's rings. These unidentified structures caused a small occultation, or shadowing, of Uranus. This meant that something, not a moon, had caused a shadow to fall across the planet. On March 14, 1977, two separate sightings confirmed that "these occultations were caused by bodies that are apparently part of a satellite belt." By March 21, 1977, there was no longer any doubt that Uranus did have rings.

Voyager 2 managed to photograph and measure all nine of the previously known rings of Uranus. It also found and photographed some new rings and not-quite-formed ringlets. From these photographs and measurements, scientists have concluded that Uranus's rings are unlike those around Saturn. In fact, they are unlike anything else seen so far.

In 1986, this image showed scientists details of parts of Uranus's known rings.

From the inner ring to the outer ring, the 13 rings identified so far are named Zeta, 6, 5, 4, Alpha, Beta, Eta, Gamma, Delta, Lambda, Epsilon, Nu, and Mu. Most of the planet's rings are narrow. They are not perfectly round, and each one varies along its length, growing slightly broader or narrower. The fact that the rings exist and have sharp

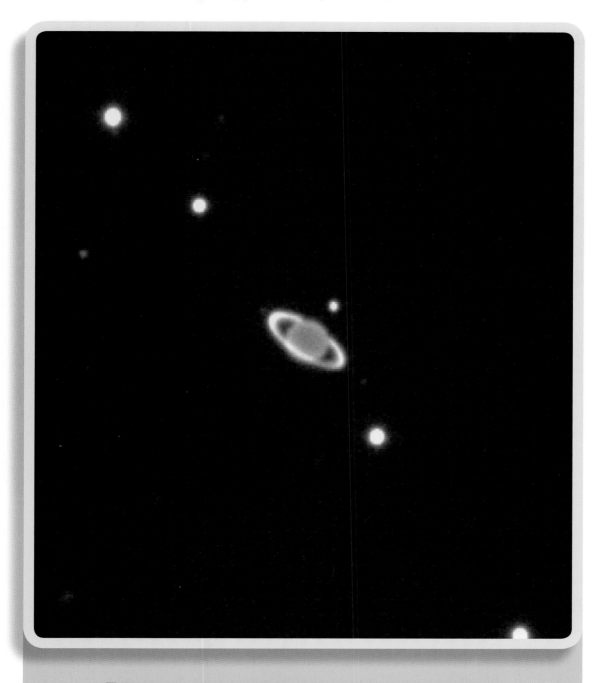

This image of a ringed Uranus and some of its moons was taken in 2002 at an observatory in Chile.

edges supports the theory that there are more tiny moonlets holding them together as Ophelia and Cordelia hold the Epsilon ring together with the force of their gravity.

As this illustration shows, scientists believe that Uranus's rings are made up of dust and particles of different size.

Incomplete Rings

Because there are so many incomplete rings and such thin main rings, scientists suspect that the entire ring system may be far younger than Uranus itself. Some of these incomplete rings are only 160 feet (50 m) wide, and some are even narrower. One theory is that the rings are particles left over from a shattered moon.

THE ATMOSPHERE

Voyager 2 made its closest approach to the planet on January 24, 1986. It sent back the first clear data about the Uranian atmosphere. As scientists on Earth had expected, the two main elements making up the atmosphere were hydrogen and helium, which are two of the most common elements in our Solar System. However, they were wrong about the amount of helium. They had calculated that there would be at least 40 percent of it in the atmosphere, but *Voyager 2* revealed only 15 percent.

That was hardly a disappointment to the scientists, however, since *Voyager* was giving them such accurate information. *Voyager 2* also relayed that there was methane in the atmospheric mix. It is the methane that makes Uranus appear blue-green, since methane does not let any red light show.

Scientists used special techniques to process this image of Uranus, giving them a better picture of what the atmosphere is made of.

This *Voyager 2* image of Uranus shows the planet's rim. Its pale blue-green color is a result of the methane in the planet's atmosphere.

SPECTROSCOPY

Astronomers knew what elements made up the Uranian atmosphere through the use of spectroscopy, which is the detailed study of light from an object—in this case, the atmosphere of Uranus. A spectrometer (the instrument that lets scientists study light) spread light from Uranus's atmosphere out into a spectrum, or rainbow. Each element, such as hydrogen, has its own "signature" spectrum. Astronomers analyzed the different spectra to determine which elements were in the Uranian atmosphere.

Voyager 2 also showed astronomers that Uranus's atmosphere is made up of bands of clouds that are similar to the bands easily seen in images of Jupiter. Like the winds on Jupiter, winds on Uranus move in the same direction in which the planet rotates. They are strong winds, ranging from 90 to 360 miles per hour (40 to 160 m per second). These are also high winds, similar to Earth's jet streams, which constantly blow at about 110 miles per hour (50 m per second).

There was also a layer of photochemical smog, a form of air pollution, around Uranus's sunlit pole. While photochemical smog on Earth is generally due to pollution from industry, on Uranus it is due to the combination of sunlight, hydrogen, and other elements. The sunlit pole also gave off its own light, reflecting from the cloud layers. Scientists called it "dayglow."

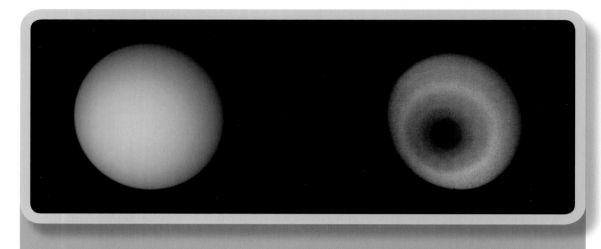

The image on the left shows how Uranus would look to humans if they could look at the planet while on *Voyager 2*. The image on the right uses special developing to show the smog particles (purple, pink, and red) that appear over one of Uranus's poles.

In addition to its observations of the planet's atmosphere, *Voyager 2* also sent back signals proving that Uranus, like the other planets, does have a magnetic field. A planet's magnetic field helps to protect it from strong **solar winds**. The strength of Uranus's magnetic field seems equal to Earth's.

A PLANET ON ITS SIDE

Voyager 2 also proved that Uranus definitely does lie almost on its side. This means that the poles are left and right, rather than top and bottom, like other planets. This odd position also makes

Uranus's magnetic field odd. Usually a magnetic field is about the same throughout. Uranus's, however, varies from point to point.

Voyager 2 also helped determine the length of a Uranian day, or the rate at which the planet turns on its axis. A day on Uranus is about seventeen hours and fourteen minutes long.

After its extensive flyby of Uranus, its moons, and its rings, *Voyager 2* received the NASA command to leave and head on to its next destination—Neptune. *Voyager 2*'s 1986 mission was the last time an Earth spacecraft visited Uranus. But studies of Uranus were far from over.

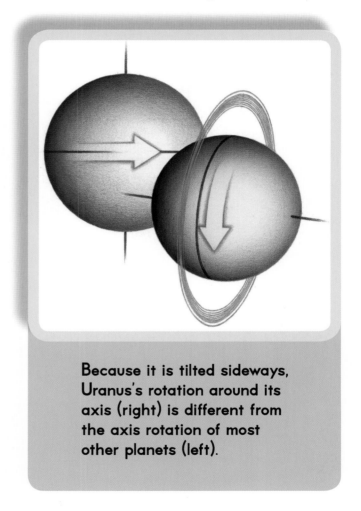

Because it is tilted sideways, Uranus's rotation around its axis (right) is different from the axis rotation of most other planets (left).

4

EXPLORING THE PLANET

here will never be manned landings on Uranus. There can be no landings at all because the planet literally has no surface on which to land. Like Jupiter, Neptune, and Saturn, Uranus is a planet that is considered a gas giant. A gas giant may have a solid rocky core, but it is primarily made up of gases that are denser, or packed tighter, near the core and less dense where its surface would be.

THE ORIGIN OF THE GAS GIANTS

Scientists have created many mathematical and computer models to try to learn how gas giants could have formed. They

This illustration shows our Solar System's four gas giants: Jupiter (bottom left), Saturn (right), Neptune (upper right), and Uranus (upper left).

believe that because the gas giants contain so much helium and hydrogen—the basic gases of space—they must have formed fairly early during the creation of this Solar System. It would have taken place when the entire new system was still surrounded by gases. As the new Solar System began to cool and contract, cores of icy chemicals would have formed. The increasing gravitational force of the cores drew the gases in. Since Jupiter and Saturn are closer to the Sun, they "grabbed" the majority of the gases, making them the two largest gas planets. Uranus, because it was so much farther from the Sun, got whatever was left. That would explain why Uranus is so much smaller than Jupiter or Saturn.

Jupiter is the largest gas giant. However, Uranus is still impressive in size. Its mass is about 14.5 times larger than Earth's. Because Uranus does not have a solid surface, calculating an accurate size for the planet is difficult, but the best measurement across its equator gives a diameter of about 31,744 miles (51,118 km).

Uranus, though, is not a typical gas giant. Scientists think that Uranus's core is a hot "soup" of water, methane, ammonia, and traces of various chemicals. This core is larger than the core of Earth by at least ten times. But *Voyager 2* was unable to pick up any signs of interior heat radiating, or spreading, out from the planet. The other gas giants release much of their heat energy, which was created from their cores. The same process most

Mercury, Venus, Earth, and Mars are the terrestrial, or land, planets. Jupiter, Saturn, Uranus, and Neptune are considered gas giants. Pluto, which was once considered a main planet alongside the others, is now known as a dwarf planet.

likely takes place within Uranus, but scientists are not certain as to why it is not showing up except in very tiny amounts of heat radiating from the planet.

AN INHOSPITABLE PLANET

The strongest Earth-based telescopes today, such as the Keck Observatory in Hawaii, show Uranus as a small, round, blue-green disk. It is so far from the Sun that it takes Uranus 84 years to complete one orbit around the Sun. It is far from hospitable—or livable—by Earth standards. Uranus's atmosphere has no oxygen, which humans need to breathe. As the *Voyager 2* revealed, the atmosphere is made up mostly of hydrogen and helium, as well as small amounts of methane, with traces of water and ammonia. This kind of atmosphere would be poisonous to humans who tried

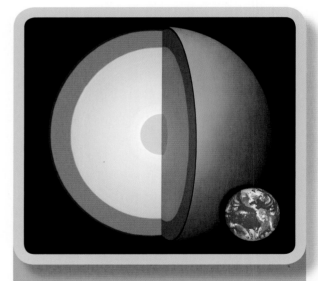

Scientists think that Uranus's core is probably made of rock, and is surrounded by layers of ice and liquid hydrogen. An illustration of Earth is shown to scale next to Uranus, displaying the difference in size.

COMPARING URANUS AND EARTH

	URANUS	EARTH
DISTANCE FROM THE SUN	2.85 billion miles (1.77 billion km)	93 million miles (149 million km)
DIAMETER	31,744 miles (51,118 km)	7,926 miles (12,756 km)
AVERAGE TEMPERATURE	-350 degrees Fahrenheit (-212 degrees Celsius)	60 degrees Fahrenheit (15 degrees C)
GRAVITY	20 percent lighter than Earth's gravity	
LENGTH OF YEAR	About 84 Earth years	365 days
LENGTH OF DAY	About 17.24 hours	24 hours
NUMBER OF MOONS	27	1
COMPOSITION OF PLANET	Hydrogen, helium, frozen water, methane, and ammonia	Mostly metals and rock
ATMOSPHERE	Mostly hydrogen and helium with small amounts of methane, ammonia, water, and other gases	Mostly nitrogen and oxygen

to breathe its air. As if the chemical makeup of the planet was not enough to keep humans from living there, Uranus's temperatures are way too cold for humans. The average temperature on Uranus is approximately -350 degrees Fahrenheit (-212 degrees C).

Humans and other Earth life-forms need water to survive. Uranus does have water, but it is either deep inside the planet or locked in ice. The water is not drinkable or usable. Water has been also been detected on some of Uranus's moons, but it is also frozen.

THE HUBBLE SPACE TELESCOPE

Twentieth-century astronomers knew that the best way to view distant objects would be from a telescope in space. Until the end of the twentieth century, that was only a dream. The Hubble Space Telescope, or HST, would change all that. Construction of the HST was completed in 1985. In 1990, the Space Shuttle *Discovery* launched with the HST onboard. Once the shuttle was in the right orbit, the astronauts carefully placed the HST into space, 347 miles (559 km) above Earth. The shuttle then slowly flew away from the telescope, leaving it in the hands of the crew on Earth who would control it remotely. Scientist manage the Hubble using computers from Earth. Sometimes, however,

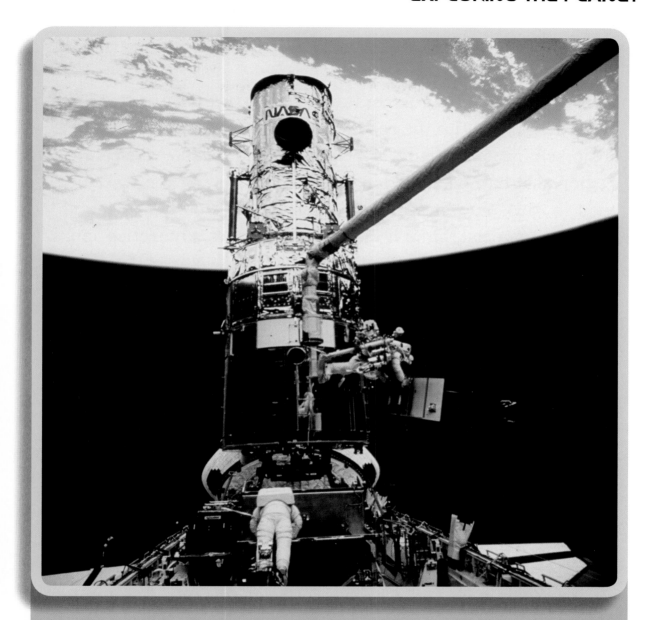

In December of 1993, astronauts from the Space Shuttle *Endeavor* made repairs to the Hubble Space Telescope. A view of Earth is shown in the background.

astronauts use shuttles to travel to the telescope to make repairs and adjustments.

In 1997, the Hubble's cameras focused on Uranus. The scientists were delighted with the results. The photographs showed some major changes. A string of brighter clouds was revealed in a region that had been hidden by darkness during the *Voyager 2* visit in 1986. There was also a clearly visible South Pole "hood" of paler material, similar to the way Earth's Antarctica looks like a white hood from outer space.

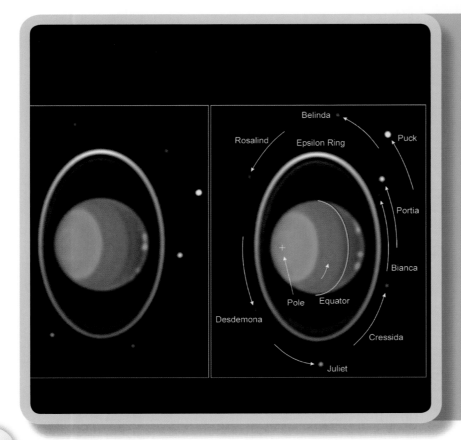

The Hubble Space Telescope took these images of Uranus in 1997. The image on the right, which was taken ninety minutes after the image on the left, showed scientists how Uranus rotated during that time.

The Seasons

On Earth, the seasons are caused by our planet's slight tilt. Because of it, our planet's Northern and Southern hemispheres are closer or farther away from the Sun as Earth moves around the Sun in a year. However, Uranus is tilted almost completely on its side. The Sun can shine directly on one pole for half of a Uranian year, which is about 42 Earth years. That causes seasons far longer than those on Earth.

In 1999, the Hubble Space Telescope revealed seasonal changes on Uranus for the first time. It showed the coming of summer, with massive storms and temperatures of -300 degrees Fahrenheit (-184 degrees C). The increasing amount of sunlight on the northern pole warmed the atmosphere and created the massive storms of a Uranian spring. This did not mean that there would be too much of a change. Even though Uranus has seasons that can last more than twenty years, the temperature differences between the summer and winter sides is less than would be expected. This is because the planet is so far from the Sun.

A movie of the changing Uranian seasons made up of a series of Hubble photographs shows a wobble in the ring system. This was possibly caused by Uranus's shape, which is like a slightly flattened globe, as well as from the gravitational pull of its many moons. Dr. Heidi Hammel, now the Co-Director of Research and Planetary Sciences at the Space Science Institute, said that, "No one has ever seen this view in the modern era of astronomy

Scientists at the W. M. Keck Observatory use powerful telescopes to explore outer space. The observatory is located at the top of the dormant, or inactive, Mauna Kea volcano in Hawaii.

because of the long year of Uranus—more than eighty-four Earth years." In 2004, the Keck Observatory in Hawaii took some very detailed images of Uranus as the planet approached its southern autumnal equinox, which is when the equator is lit by the Sun.

New Moons and Rings

More Hubble images focused on Uranus in 2005. They revealed two more moons and two more rings. The new moons were named Mab and Cupid. This brought the new number of Uranus's moons up to twenty-seven.

In 2007 and 2008, Earth's orbit around the Sun gave astronomers three chances to view the rings of Uranus. As of now, there are no NASA missions planned to Uranus. These will have to wait for the future when there will be cheaper and more efficient spacecraft.

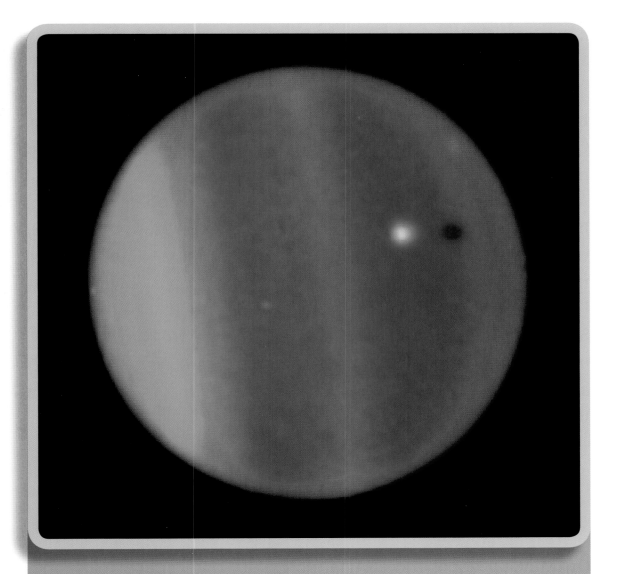

The Hubble Space Telescope has provided scientists with amazing photographs of Uranus and its moons. This image, taken in 2006, shows the moon Ariel (white dot) as it orbits Uranus. The image is so clear that Ariel's shadow can be seen on the cloud surface of Uranus.

THE EUROPEAN SPACE AGENCY

NASA, however, is not the only space organization on Earth. Other nations also have their own space programs. Often, these programs work with NASA on space missions.

The European Space Agency (ESA) was established in 1975. It is a multinational organization that is dedicated, like NASA, to the exploration of space. Eighteen nations are taking part in the ESA. They are France, the Czech Republic, Germany, Italy, the United Kingdom, Belgium, Spain, the Netherlands, Sweden, Switzerland, Austria, Denmark, Norway, Finland, Ireland, Portugal, Greece, and Luxembourg. More nations, such as Hungary, Romania, and Poland, may also join in the near future.

THE HERSCHEL SPACE OBSERVATORY

On May 14, 2009, the ESA launched its own space telescope, which was named the Herschel Space Observatory in honor of William Herschel. To make the trip more cost-effective, the ESA launched Herschel together with Planck, a mission to study the cosmic microwave background **radiation** over the entire sky.

This photograph from 2008 shows scientists and engineers adjusting different parts of the Herschel Space Observatory as it is built and prepared for its 2009 launch.

The two spacecraft separated soon after launch and are designed to operate independently.

The ESA is listing four main objectives for the Herschel Space Observatory. One is to study the formation of galaxies in the early universe and their evolution. The observatory will also investigate the creation of stars. Observations will be taken of the chemical composition of the atmospheres and surfaces of comets, planets, and satellites. The molecular chemistry, or basic chemical makeup, of the universe is also one of the observatory's main missions.

The Herschel Space Observatory is the largest **infrared** space observatory ever launched. It stands approximately 24 feet (7.5 m) high and 14 feet (4 m) wide. It has a launch weight of more than 7 tons (3.3 tonnes).

The spacecraft is made up of a service module and a payload module. The service module holds the systems for power conditioning, altitude control, data handling, and communications, together with the parts of the scientific instruments that need to be kept warm. The payload module consists of the telescope and the parts of the instruments that need to stay cool, such as the sensitive detector units and cooling systems. The payload module is fitted with a sunshield that protects the telescope from sunlight or the Sun's normal radiation, although it does carry solar cells that draw energy from the Sun to generate power for the observatory. The shield also keeps light from Earth from entering the telescope and distorting the images it views.

Seeing in the Infrared

Human eyes cannot see into the infrared. That is a band of light just past the red spectrum. There is a good reason to use a telescope that can see into the infrared and then translate what it sees into images that humans can see. Much of the universe is just too cold to radiate light in a way that humans can normally see. The only way to study such cold objects is by looking at them in the infrared spectrum. The Herschel Observatory will be able do this with ease.

There is another reason why astronomers want a telescope that can see into the infrared. Many objects they want to know more about are hiding in or behind clouds of space gas or dust.

For example, stars and planets being "born" are hidden within the clouds of dust and gas out of which they are being created. Infrared searches can see through much of the dust.

In addition to viewing other planets and celestial bodies in outer space, it is likely that the observatory will turn its sights on Uranus. With studies done this time in the infrared, who knows how much more we will learn about Uranus's chemistry, moons, and rings. More than two hundred years after its discovery, Uranus may finally reveal some of its mysteries to astronomers.

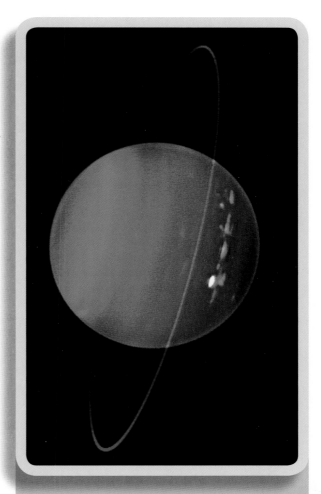

Infrared images, such as this one taken from a telescope in Hawaii in 2004, allow scientists to see detailed features of Uranus, such as the clouds above the planet's atmosphere (white and light blue spots).

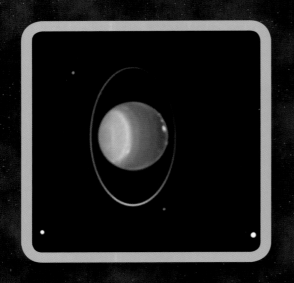

QUICK FACTS ABOUT URANUS

YEAR OF DISCOVERY: 1781

DISCOVERER: William Herschel

SOURCE OF NAME: Ancient Greek god of the sky

TYPE OF PLANET: Gas giant

DIAMETER: 31,744 miles (51,118 km)—more than four times that of Earth

AVERAGE DISTANCE FROM THE SUN: 2.85 billion miles (1.77 billion km)

AVERAGE DISTANCE FROM EARTH: 1.6 billion miles (2.57 billion km)

AVERAGE TEMPERATURE: -350 degrees Fahrenheit (-212 degrees C)

LENGTH OF YEAR: About 84 Earth years

LENGTH OF DAY: About 17.24 Earth hours

MOONS: Twenty-seven known moons: Cordelia, Ophelia, Bianca, Cressida, Desdemona, Juliet, Portia, Rosalind, Mab, Belinda, Perdita, Puck, Cupid, Miranda, Francisco, Ariel, Umbriel, Titania, Oberon, Caliban, Stephano, Trinculo, Sycorax, Margaret, Prospero, Setebos, Ferdinand

GLOSSARY

asteroids—Small, rocky objects that have no atmosphere. They usually orbit the Sun or the planets.

astronomer—Someone who studies space and celestial bodies and forces.

astronomy—The study of space and celestial bodies and forces.

atmosphere—All the gases that surround a planet or a star.

axis—An imaginary line that runs through the center of a planet. A planet rotates around its axis.

crust—The outermost layer of a planet or a moon.

fault lines—Cracks or breaks in the surface of a planet or moon that are usually signs of geological activity beneath the surface.

geologic—Having to do with the study of a planet's or celestial body's natural features and the forces that shaped them.

gravity—The force that attracts objects to each other. The force of gravity increases as objects come closer together and decreases the farther apart they are.

infrared— A band of light past the red end of the spectrum that humans cannot see.

NASA—The National Aeronautics and Space Administration is the official space agency of the United States.

nebula—An immense cloud of dust and gas molecules in outer space.

orbit—The path something takes around another planet, a celestial body, or the Sun.

radiation—Energy that is given off by an object.

satellite—An object—natural or human-made—that orbits a celestial body. For example, Uranus's moons are natural satellites that orbit the planet.

solar wind—A steady stream of gas particles from the Sun's atmosphere.

spectrum—A range of color like that seen in a rainbow or a prism.

FIND OUT MORE

BOOKS

Aguilar, David. *Planets, Stars, and Galaxies: A Visual Encyclopedia of Our Universe.* Washington, D.C.: National Geographic Society, 2007.

Barnes-Svarney, Patricia. *A Traveler's Guide to the Solar System.* New York, NY: Sterling Publishing, 2008.

Birch, Robin. *Uranus.* New York: Chelsea House Publishers, 2008.

Goss, Tim. *The Universe: The Outer Planets.* Chicago: Heinemann Library, 2008.

Slade, Suzanne. *A Look at Uranus.* New York: PowerKids Press, 2008.

WEBSITES

CoolCosmos: Uranus
http://coolcosmos.ipac.caltech.edu/cosmic_kids/AskKids/uranus.shtml

Curious about Astronomy? Ask an Astronomer
http://curious.astro.cornell.edu

HubbleSite
http://hubblesite.org

Huge Spring Storms Rouse Uranus from Winter Hibernation
http://hubblesite.org/newscenter/archive/releases/1999/11/video/b/

NASA Kids' Club
http://www.nasa.gov/audience/forkids/kidsclub/flash/index.html

NASA Solar System Exploration for Kids
http://solarsystem.nasa.gov/kids/index.cfm

NASA Space Place: Voyagers 1 and 2
http://spaceplace.nasa.gov/en/kids/vgr_fact3.shtml

NASA: Uranus
  http://www.nasa.gov/worldbook/uranus_worldbook.html

Uranus
  http://kids.nineplanets.org/uranus.htm

BIBLIOGRAPHY

The author found these resources especially helpful when researching this book.

Corfield, Richard. *Lives of the Planets: A Natural History of the Solar System.* New York: Basic Books, 2007.

International Astronomical Union Circular. "Occultations by Uranus and (6) Hebe." http://www.cfa.harvard.edu/iauc/03000/03047.html

---. "8213." http://www.cfa.harvard.edu/iauc/08200/08213.html

---. "Satellites of Uranus." http://www.cfa.harvard.edu/iauc/08600/08648.html

---. "Ring of Uranus." http://www.cfa.harvard.edu/iauc/08800/08826.html

Jet Propulsion Laboratory—California Institute of Technology. "Uranus." http://www.jpl.nasa.gov/solar_system/planets/uranus_index.html

Miller, Ron, and William K. Hartmann. *The Grand Tour: A Traveler's Guide to the Solar System.* New York: Workman Publishing, 2005.

Price, Fred W. *The Planet Observer's Handbook.* New York: Cambridge University Press, 2000.

Sobel, Dava. *The Planets.* New York: Viking, 2005.

INDEX

Page numbers in **boldface** indicate photos or illustrations.

ABOUT THE AUTHOR

Josepha Sherman has written everything from fantasy novels to science books to short articles about quantum mechanics for elementary-school students.